Sports Illustrated KIDS
BASEBALL RECORDS SMASHED!

by Bruce Berglund

CAPSTONE PRESS
a capstone imprint

Published by Capstone Press, an imprint of Capstone
1710 Roe Crest Drive, North Mankato, Minnesota 56003
capstonepub.com

Library of Congress Cataloging-in-Publication Data
Names: Berglund, Bruce R. author.
Title: Baseball records smashed! / by Bruce Berglund.
Description: North Mankato, Minnesota : Capstone Press, [2024] | Series: Sports illustrated kids. Record smashers | Includes bibliographical references and index. | Audience: Ages 9–11 | Audience: Grades 4–6 | Summary: "In baseball, long games are marked by spectacular moments—like Nolan Ryan beating Sandy Koufax's no-hitter record or Ichiro Suzuki smashing George Sisler's record number of hits in a season. In this Sports Illustrated Kids book, young readers can experience record-breaking plays in baseball. Fast-paced and fact-filled, this collection of record smashers will delight sports fans with thrilling feats in baseball history"—Provided by publisher.
Identifiers: LCCN 2023000019 (print) | LCCN 2023000020 (ebook) | ISBN 9781669049876 (hardcover) | ISBN 9781669049838 (eBook PDF) | ISBN 9781669049852 (kindle edition) | ISBN 9781669049869 (epub)
Subjects: LCSH: Baseball—Records—United States—Juvenile literature. | Baseball—United States—History—Juvenile literature.
Classification: LCC GV877 .B46 2024 (print) | LCC GV877 (ebook) | DDC 796.357021—dc23/eng/20230112
LC record available at https://lccn.loc.gov/2023000019
LC ebook record available at https://lccn.loc.gov/2023000020

Editorial Credits
Editor: Ericka Smith; Designer: Terri Poburka; Media Researcher: Svetlana Zhurkin; Production Specialist: Katy LaVigne

Image Credits
Alamy: Ewing Galloway, 26, Glasshouse Images, 11, ZUMA Wire/Dick Druckman, 9; Associated Press: Ed Kolenovsky, 14, File/Ray Stubblebine, 22, Fort Worth Star-Telegram/Jerry Hoefer, 17, Kathy Willens, 8, Mark J. Terrill, cover (front), SF, 16, Tim Johnson, 15; Getty Images: Allsport/Ezra Shaw, 19, Andrew D. Bernstein, 24, Focus on Sport, 25, General Photographic Agency, 5, Jonathan Daniel, 10, Lisa Blumenfeld, 13, Patrick McDermott, 18, 20–21, Ronald Martinez, 27, 28, Steph Chambers, 29, Toronto Star/Mike Slaughter, 23; Shutterstock: Eugene Onischenko, cover (back), krissikunterbunt (fireworks), cover and throughout, pixssa (cracked background), 1 and throughout; Sports Illustrated: Erick W. Rasco, 6, 7

TABLE OF CONTENTS

Words in **bold** are in the glossary.

RECORDS OLD AND NEW

Baseball records go back a long time. Some Major League Baseball (MLB) records are more than a hundred years old.

Today's players are smashing records—new and old. That's part of the fun. Here are some of baseball's greatest record-breaking moments.

FACT

Babe Ruth was one of MLB's earliest record breakers. In 1919, he broke the record of 16 home runs in one season by hitting 29 homers.

Babe Ruth

RECORD-SMASHING ROOKIES

Some records take a long time to break. Others are broken quickly.

In 2017, Yankees player Aaron Judge smashed the record for most home runs by a **rookie**. He hit 52 homers. He broke Mark McGwire's record of 49 homers. It had lasted 30 years.

Judge hitting a home run in 2017

Pete Alonso

But Judge's record lasted only two years. In 2019, Mets rookie Pete Alonso hit homers all season. With three days left in the regular season, Alonso tied Judge's record. The next night, fans packed the stadium to see if Alonso would break it.

Smash! Alonso hit a homer and set a new record—53 homers by a rookie.

Alonso celebrating 53 homers

A LOT OF HITS

Pete Alonso broke a new record. Ichiro Suzuki smashed one that was 84 years old.

In 1920, George Sisler set the record for most hits in a season. For decades, no batter came close to his 257 hits. In 2004, Ichiro changed that.

Ichiro Suzuki

George Sisler

That year, Ichiro started the season cold. Eventually, he began hitting. In some games, he would have five hits.

During a game on October 1, 2004, Ichiro got a single in the first inning to tie Sisler's record. In the third inning, he broke it. Ichiro ended the season with 262 hits.

FACT

Only seven players in MLB history have 250 or more hits in a season.

NO HITS

In baseball, some records seem unbeatable—like Nolan Ryan's record for most **no-hitters**.

In 1975, Ryan tied Sandy Koufax's old record of four no-hitters. In 1981, he finally smashed it with his fifth no-hitter.

Nolan Ryan

Ryan waving to the crowd after his fifth no-hitter

But Ryan wasn't done yet. In 1990, he pitched his sixth no-hitter. The next season, Ryan got his seventh no-hitter! He struck out the Blue Jays' Roberto Alomar to end the game.

Ryan after his seventh no-hitter

CLOSING THE WINS

Mariano Rivera was a feared **closer** for the Yankees. He usually saved the win for his team.

Mariano Rivera

In 2011, Rivera smashed the record for saves by a closer. In a game against the Twins, the Yankees had a big lead early in the game, but the Twins came back. With the Yankees leading 6–4, Rivera pitched the ninth inning.

Rivera (right) celebrating a win with his teammates

Rivera got three batters out in a row. He struck out the last batter in only three pitches. He set a new record—602 career saves!

Rivera **retired** two years later with 652 saves.

Rivera was an even better pitcher in the playoffs and the World Series. He pitched 141 innings in postseason games—and allowed only 13 runs.

BASEBALL'S GREATEST THIEF

Rickey Henderson was baseball's best base stealer. When he got on base, he would say, "Rickey's gotta go!" And off he went.

Henderson running to steal a base

Runners usually steal second base. Most don't steal third base. But Henderson did.

Henderson sliding into third base

When Henderson stole third base on May 1, 1991, the catcher's throw wasn't even close. Henderson lifted the base over his head to celebrate. He had just racked up 939 stolen bases. He smashed Lou Brock's 1979 record!

Henderson celebrating 939 steals

Henderson played 12 more seasons. He retired with 1,406 stolen bases. No other MLB player has more than 1,000 stolen bases.

SMASHING RECORDS, MAKING HISTORY

When Babe Ruth played, all pitchers took their turn batting. In 1919, Ruth pitched 133 innings and struck out 30 batters. He also hit 29 homers.

Ruth batting in 1934

Shohei Ohtani pitches and hits like no player since the Babe. When he joined the Angels in 2018, he was the only MLB pitcher who was also a **designated hitter**.

Shohei Ohtani

In 2021, Ohtani pitched 130 innings and struck out 156 batters. At the plate, Ohtani knocked 46 homers. He shattered Ruth's record for most homers and strikeouts by one player.

There's no other MLB player like Ohtani—a great pitcher and a great batter. Keep watching to see how many records he will smash!

Ohtani hitting a homer

GLOSSARY

closer (KLOH-zuhr)—the pitcher who comes in at the end of a baseball game when their team is ahead to make sure the other team does not score

designated hitter (DEZ-ig-nay-tid HIT-ur)—a player who hits for pitchers

no-hitter (no-HIT-ur)—a game in which one team does not allow the other team to get a hit

retire (ri-TIRE)—to give up work usually because of a person's age

rookie (RUK-ee)—a player who is playing their first year on a team

READ MORE

Berglund, Bruce. *Football Records Smashed!* North Mankato, MN: Capstone, 2024.

Driscoll, Martin. *Baseball Talk: Grand Slam, Frozen Rope, and More Big-League Lingo.* North Mankato, MN: Capstone, 2023.

Martin, Andrew. *Baseball's Greatest Players: 10 Baseball Biographies for New Readers*. Emeryville, CA: Rockridge Press, 2022.

INTERNET SITES

America's Library: Hall of Fame Pitchers
americaslibrary.gov/jp/bball/jp_bball_pitch_1.html

Baseball Reference: Overall Baseball Leaders & Baseball Records
baseball-reference.com/leaders

Major League Baseball: MLB Kids
mlb.com/fans/kids

INDEX

ABOUT THE AUTHOR

Bruce Berglund played baseball, hockey, and football as a kid. When he got older, he was a coach and referee. Bruce taught college history for many years. He wrote a history book for adults on world hockey. He is now writing a book about the history of referees and umpires.